MATCHED

How to Get Girls on Tinder, Bumble

or Any Other Dating App or Website

By Zac Miller

ISBN: 9781073149049
Published by ZML Corp LLC

Table of Contents

Disclaimer

This book is written for informational and entertainment purposes only. None of this book should be considered legal advice. It is illegal to copy or distribute any part of this book with written consent from the author or publisher. If you choose to do so, I will contact my attorney who will take you to jail. I regularly and actively search the internet for individuals infringing on my copyright.

This Page Intentionally Left Blank

Introduction

Times have changed! Gone are the days where you go down to your local watering hole to meet a girl. The internet has given rise to a much better dating experience in the form of dating apps. Apps like Tinder, Bumble, and Coffee Meets Bagels have taken the millennial generation by storm. But with any new technology comes a learning curve. And when you factor in women, this learning curve becomes exponential. Below I have a picture of the official guide to understanding women.

Fortunately for you, I've already read it all. Hi, my name is Zac Miller and I want to help you in your journey with women. In this book I will teach you how to talk to, attract, and go out with girls on any dating app you are using. Due to Tinder being the most popular, many examples in this book will be specific towards Tinder, however these examples can be applied across all platforms.

Some of the premises in this book overlap with my first book *The Art of the Text* (**linkpony.com/text**). That is because of the similarity when it comes to messaging girls on Tinder and texting girls. If you haven't already, I highly suggest reading my first book, as it will give you a deeper background into my philosophy, and a better understanding of the reasons behind my advice in this book.

You can also learn more about me, more books I have written, and free advice related to attracting girls on my website, GetMoreDates.com.

I also have a "VIP Coaching" section where we can talk over the phone and email. Here I can provide you with more personalized advice to help you attract women.

Part 1
Your Profile

Your profile is the most important aspect of everything when it comes to online dating. A few pictures and a brief summary of your life is all the girl has to judge you by, so you have to make it compelling to garner that right swipe. Something you need to understand about girls on Tinder is they are receiving messages from A LOT of guys. In one experiment I conducted, I set up a fake Tinder profile with a girl fitting a 7 out of 10 attractiveness profile. I'd say about 80% of the guys I right swiped matched with me. Think about that! As a decent looking guy, you're lucky to get 1 out of 20. This girl was literally getting eight out of every ten guys I right swiped on, and she was a 7! Imagine had she instead been a perfect 10! What I'm trying to convey is there is **A TON** of competition for girls on dating apps, and for most guys, the girls are the choosers. For this reason, your profile has to stand out from the other guys.

Now I'm not saying to go out, rent a Lamborghini, and take pictures of yourself laying on the hood. You don't want to be someone you're not, because when you pick her up in your Corolla for the date, that will be a tough explanation. What I'm saying is to display the best side of yourself in your profile, and maybe stretch the truth a little if you need to.

Considering your pictures are one of the few things this girl has to judge you by, we are going to need to talk about appearance. Looks are one of the main aspects of dating apps. Besides the brief description of yourself in your bio, looks are all this girl has to judge you by. And she's not going to even read your bio if she doesn't like the way you look. For this reason, you want to appear attractive to these girls. Remember, you are competing with a large number of other guys, and the king of the jungle is the one who gets the girl. Here are some relatively quick and inexpensive ways to improve your appearance.

Get a Nice Hair Style

If you've been doing the buzz cut since you were 8, now may be a good time to try something new. Styles change with the times. A good idea is to go to a local stylist, and tell them you want to try out a new hairstyle and ask for their opinion. They will be happy to help you, will be familiar with the popular hair styles, and will be able to choose a style that fits with your hair type.

Whiten Your Teeth

Crest Whitestrips go for about $30 at Walmart and the results last well over a year. This is an easy way to look more attractive.

Straighten Your Teeth

A smile can go a long way. If you currently don't have great teeth, it's okay. You no longer have to pay thousands of dollars at an orthodontist, as times are a changing. There are a few direct to home, teeth adjustment companies that will help you with this, such as the one here: **linkpony.com/smile**. The average treatment length is just six months, and they allow you to make monthly payments if you are strapped for cash. This is a small price to pay to have a perfect smile that will last a lifetime, and will up your attractiveness to females exponentially. I can't tell you the number of girls who love a great smile.

New Wardrobe

If your wardrobe is on the old side, now is a good time to update it. Go to TJ Maxx or Ross and get some new clothes which you can wear in your photos. This is another easy, inexpensive way to improve your appearance.

Build Muscle

Most girls are into a guy with a muscular body. Just like guys are attracted to T & A, girls are attracted to muscles. Blame it on evolution, or aliens or whatever you want to, but it's just the way it is. For this reason, getting a little more muscular will be beneficial when it comes to attracting girls. A study done at Harvard found women preferred men with muscles and wide shoulders, with the most attractive male body type being an upside down triangle. As in broad shoulders and a slim waist. I have an example below.

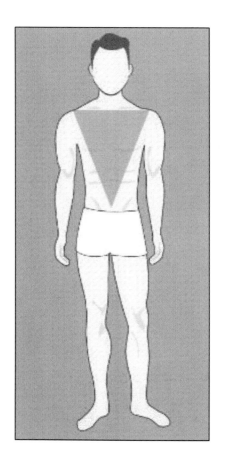

Now when I say muscular, I'm not talking Macho Man Randy Savage, as there is a point when you have too much muscle. However most women prefer muscles on men. The "Athlean-X" channel on YouTube (linkpony.com/athlean) and Bodybuilding.com are two great places for tips on building muscle.

I recently saw an app which allows you to morph your body to look like a bodybuilder with six pack abs and huge muscles. Please do not use any apps like this. When you meet your dates and your six pack is gone, your date will be gone soon too. Like I said, you can stretch the truth a little, but don't take it over board.

Pictures

It used to be six, but now the nine pictures Tinder allows is all this girl has to judge you by. The first picture is the absolutely most important, and within just a couple seconds, this girl will decide if she wants to start talking to you or if you're going into her left swipe pile. Many girls do not go past the first picture or even read the bio if they don't like what they see in the first image. You need to put the best picture of yourself you can. I want to reiterate you have competition and a lot of it. There are so many guys on Tinder and girls have their choice. You need to stand out from the pack. For this reason, I highly suggest getting professional pictures taken of yourself. Whether you know someone with a nice camera or you hire a freelance photographer, these professional photos will make your profile stand out.

Bring a few outfits with you, and have multiple pictures of yourself taken in different backgrounds. You just need to do this once. Sure it may cost you a little bit of your time and money, but it will pay generous dividends when it comes to how many matches you get. You will stand out from the other guys who are taking selfies in the mirror. Have your photographer take a TON of photos of you during the session, as you most likely will only like a few of them.

Not all the pictures in your profile need to be professionally taken, but the first one should be. In terms of the other pictures, it's a good idea to use photos where someone else has taken it, as in NOT selfies. No matter the situation, selfies are always worse than a photo someone else has taken for you. My recommendation is to not having any selfies on your Tinder profile. And speaking of selfies, mirror selfies are a sin and should be discontinued immediately. Whether it be at the gym, in your bathroom, or anywhere else, you want to stay away from selfies, and especially mirror selfies on your profile; many girls are turned off by this. It screams douche like a blow horn on a lighthouse.

If you have a nice body, put a picture of yourself at the pool or out on a boat that someone else has taken. This looks much more natural, and doesn't appear like you're trying as hard. If you don't have a nice body, it's best to skip the beach picture. Also, make sure you have at least 2 pictures of your entire body. I'm sure you've seen the girls who have 9 pictures of their face at different angles. This conveys that you're trying to hide something, and girls don't like when guys do this either. So while some close ups of your face are fine, make sure to include some pictures of your entire body. Like men, women have their preferences and they want to see your whole body.

Picture Tips

Studies show that certain aspects of a man's photo can increase the probability of attracting a woman. One is not smiling.

In a study performed in 2011 at the University of British Columbia, men where perceived as *less sexually attractive* when they smiled. In the photo on the next page, the section on the left shows this man with a straight face; the section on the right shows the same man with a smile.

Take some pictures of yourself on your phone and look at both. I think you'll be surprised how effective this is. And while this study isn't a concrete fact, it still should be taken into consideration. Now you don't want to not smile in all your photos, as you may look like a serial killer, but in some of your photos, rock the straight face.

Another attractive trait is a slight squint, which has been called a "squinch." Studies find others find you more attractive when you squinch, versus being wide eyed, as it displays confidence. Staring wide eyed into the camera comes off as uncertain and fearful. Let me show you an example.

The man on the left has a wide eyed look, while the man on the right is "squincing." Notice the difference? Being a heterosexual male, I can easily tell the guy on the right looks more attractive and confident.

One more item which you want to allocate for is symmetry. People with more symmetrical faces are deemed as more attractive by their peers. Let me show you an example:

While this photo of course displays a rather large difference, showing a man with a misshaped forehead, it proves a point of how much you notice an asymmetrical face. And while there's not much you can do if you have a misshapen forehead, you can make other aspects of your face more symmetrical such as your beard and eyebrows. This will in turn make you more attractive.

For the first picture I would suggest a professional, full body picture in which you squinch and don't smile. This first photo should be you by yourself, not with other people. And if any of your photos are with other people, especially girls, crop them out of the photo. Girls don't want to see you hugging on other girls when they are looking for a man to date. Most of your photos should be you by yourself. I'm sure you've seen the girls who have 9 photos of themselves with 5 other girls. You don't want people playing where's Waldo on your Tinder profile.

While you of course want to use the best photo you have for your profile picture, you may not know which one to choose. I suggest using a website called photofeeler.com. Here you can put a picture of yourself up, and people will rate it for you. I would suggest placing a few pictures of yourself on this website, and then using the one which gets the highest rating as your profile picture on Tinder.

Tinder and Bumble allow you to place your Instagram pictures into your profile; this is a personal choice. Having more pictures of yourself is a plus, but that's only if those are quality pictures. If your Instagram photos include the likes of you passed out drunk in your boxers, it would be best not to add your Instagram to Tinder. But if you have good photos of yourself on Instagram, I would definitely include it.

Bio

After a girl has decided that your picture is to her liking, there is a good chance she will read your bio. It's always better to have something in your bio than to have nothing. A few things you don't want to put in your bio are "disqualifiers." These are items which would exclude certain girls from matching with you. Examples of disqualifiers are:

- *"I don't know why I'm here. My friend made me make a Tinder."*

- *"I only like blondes."*

- *"If you don't like dogs, swipe left."*

While you may not be a fan of dogs, disqualifiers in profiles are poor. You are alienating potential girls that could have been extremely attractive and good matches for you. Maybe this girl doesn't like dogs now, but things could change in the future. It's just best not to have any disqualifiers in your bio.

The bio is an area for you to sell yourself. I like to keep mine a little funny, such as saying "we can tell people we met at the library." Put some hobbies you have, where you've lived, your occupation, and anything else unique about yourself. Sometimes girls will message you first, and this gives them something to talk with you about. A great item to put in your bio is "two truths and a lie." This is an instant conversation starter with girls who decide to message you first. Then girls can guess which one of the three items you put down is a lie, and it gives you both something to talk about.

Part 2
How to Increase Matches

As you are already aware, matching with girls is just the first step and is not a guarantee of success. However you cannot talk to a girl unless you match with her, so we have to start somewhere. If you're having problems getting matches, there are two possible issues:

1. You live in an area that is densely populated

2. You are trying to match with girls who may be "out of your league."

While your biography does matters, I didn't mention it as a reason you're "not getting matches," and here's why. Tinder, Bumble, and all the other online dating apps and websites are almost all based on looks. That's the first thing people are going to judge you by, and the only thing between you and a right swipe. There was a study recently conducted where a fake profile was made with a very attractive male model. I want to share this study with it, as it helps to better explain some of the types of girls on Tinder and other dating apps.

In this study, which was conducted on Tinder, a very attractive male model had a little bit of a dark past, which he placed right out in the open on his bio.

As shown in the photo on the next page, the model talks about how he just got out of prison because he had been convicted of molesting multiple children. He then goes on to say he's on Tinder because "maybe if I f*** some of you sluts I'll stop wanting to be with kids."

So here we have a convicted child molester with an absolutely vial profile, that couldn't be any more offensive. Would you believe that this guy still got matches… and a lot of them! He had girls saying things like "it's okay, I forgive you" and "everyone makes mistakes." They were still willing to talk to this disgusting guy because he was attractive. While I understand not all girls are like this, it does show how big of a factor looks are on dating apps. No matter what is in your bio, if you look attractive, you will get matches. A link to the study can be found below if you would like to read it in entirety: **linkpony.com/model**

Ray, 23

◎ less than a kilometre away.

Aspiring model. Watch out for me in GQ in a couple years ;)

You should know I've had trouble with the law my whole life. Convicted three times for rape of a child (R.O.A.C) and once for sexual activity with a child but tbf she turned 16 like a week later so it was super unfair but w/e.

I'm on tinder cause maybe if I fuck some of you sluts I'll stop wanting to be with kids (unlikely lmao, they're way tighter than your beef curtain cunts). I hope you can therefore forgive me for my past crimes.

My anthem

Young Love
◉ Kip Moore

If you've done all you can and find you are still running out of girls to match with, you have a few options:

1. Extend Your Filters - search in a larger radius or a larger age range. If you can get your search radius to include a big city near you, this will increase your match opportunities 10 fold.

2. Move - moving to an area with a larger population will greatly increase the number of girls who you can match with. Also, in larger cities, you have a better chance of receiving a reciprocal match back due to the sheer number of people.

3. Delete and Reopen Your Account - when you left swipe on someone, they will no longer show as a potential match in the future. The only way to see left swipes in the future is if either you, or the girl who you swiped left on, deletes your Tinder account, and then reopens it.

4. Lower Your Standards – based on what history has shown, 5's get with 5's, 7's get with 7's, and 10's get with 10's. It's just how human attraction works. There are of course factors such as money, power, and fame which can skew these numbers, but for the most part people are able to get into relationship with others who are around their same attractiveness level. For this reason, if you are a 7, but you only swipe right on 10's, you're most likely not going to have much success on Tinder. A better option would be to lower your standards a little and broaden your dating pool. Maybe come down to 9's and 8's. This will give you many more matches than you are currently getting if your standards are too high.

5. Up Your Attractiveness – Your last option if you are not getting many matches is to become more attractive yourself. As stated before, a big aspect of online dating is looks. Yes, girls will read your bio after they have decided you look good enough to start talking to. If you want to match with better looking girls, you may have to become better looking yourself. The tips located in Part 1, particularly building muscle, will be beneficial for you here.

Super Likes

Many guys are unaware of this feature; I know I was. At first glance, the "super like" feature seems like a new way for stalkers to work on their victims. But after closer inspection, and reading more about its use, it turns out to be a very useful feature. Bumble and other dating apps having similar "super like" capabilities, with different names. In the past, all you could do on Tinder was swipe right or left, and then hope your right swipes would match with you. If you lived in a large area, there could be potentially hundreds of guys who had swiped right on the same girl before you did, thus putting you way back in the line. The girl may have eventually gotten to your picture, but she may not have. She may have deleted her Tinder or started talking to another guy before she ever reached you, never knowing that you would have been great for her. This is where the super like comes into play.

When you super like a girl, she immediately gets a notification that she has been super liked, which is going to pique her curiosity. You are then placed in about the 3rd or 4th position in her queue, so when she gets back on Tinder, she will only have to swipe a few times before reaching your profile and deciding if she would like to match with you or not. I guarantee you this one tip alone will get you at least 3x as many matches as you were getting before.

Currently Tinder Plus, which costs $7 a month, allows you to have 5 super likes a day. You can also buy them individually, with the best price being 60 super likes for $40. If you're short on cash, the best strategy is to sign up for Tinder Plus for $7 a month, and then use the 5 super likes you get each day. Save this for the girls you find very attractive and really want to meet, considering you only get 5 a day and not all of them will match back.

Many girls will list their Snapchat ID in their

profile. If you see this, don't waste a super like, but instead add her on Snapchat. As we'll go over later in the book, having her Snapchat ID is better than only being able to message her on Tinder, as most girls are much more active on Snapchat, and you are able to see when she reads your messages. After adding said girl, send her a message with a photo of yourself (preferably the professional photo you had taken). Here would be an example:

"Hey Sarah. I saw you on Tinder and wanted to say hi. My name is Zac (include photo of yourself)"

Then when she replies, use the techniques I go over in part 4 of this book to start conversing with her. Again, having a Snapchat ID to start with is a great scenario, as you are able to skip a step in "The Tinder Staircase" I list in part 4.

As a **token of appreciation** to my readers, I am giving away my special report above titled, *Subconscious Attraction: 3 Techniques That Will Attract Her Subconsciously* **absolutely free!** Just copy the link below into your browser, put in your e-mail address, and it will be immediately sent to you.

Linkpony.com/attract

Part 3
Types of Guys and Girls on Tinder

Before we go over how to talk to girls, I want to talk about some of the more typical types of guys and girls who can be found on Tinder and other dating apps.

Types of Tinder Girls

There are mainly two types of girls who you will encounter on Tinder, which you may already be very familiar with.

The first type we'll call "Attention Seeking Girl" (ASG). This girl may have not gotten the attention she needed as a child, and is now on a dating app trying to get it from random guys. ASG is usually young, fairly good looking, and may put her Snapchat ID in her bio, as well as her Venmo ID asking for money. ASG has no intentions of actually meeting a guy, but instead wants to be told how hot she is and constantly receive messages from guys drooling over her. If you match with her, she may talk to you a little while, but eventually drops off when things start getting a little more serious. There is nothing you can do to get an ASG out on a date, as their whole motive is to just get attention. They may change their attitude in the future, but currently they stick to their motive.

The second type of girl is one in which you actually want to talk to. We'll call her "Actually Looking for a Man Girl" (ALFAMG). The look and age can vary for an ALFAMG. They'll usually have a nice bio which lists their hobbies, music taste, etc. While the types of replies received from this girl will differ, she usually does get back to you, talk to you, and ask you questions. She is generally interested in getting to know you, and potentially wants to meet you. ALFAMG is looking for a boyfriend, and wants to eventually be in a serious relationship.

While there are other types of girls on dating apps, such as just wanting to have sex girl (JWHSG), tranny girl (TG), etc. we'll just be going over the two types mentioned previously as they are the most common. Ultimately you want to try to weed out the ASG, and find the ALFAMG. You can usually tell who the ASGs are just by looking at their profile. While there is no harm in talking to an ASG, just know that it is very hard to get them onto dates, and it is not your fault if they don't commit. You did nothing wrong, it's just part of their personality.

Types of Tinder Guys

Now we'll go over the most common types of guys whom girls encounter on Tinder and other dating apps.

Boring Conversation Guy (BCG)

This guy usually starts off one of his messages with:

- *Hey*
- *What's up*
- *How you doing*

The girl may or may not respond. If she does respond, he immediately replies back with another boring response. Let's go through an example conversation:

BCG: *Hey*
Girl: *Hello*
BCG: *What's up?*
Girl: *nm, just at my house. You?*
BCG: *yeah same, just watching TV*

Then possibly later that night, or the next morning he may text her again, the cycle repeats itself. BCG doesn't have much luck on dating apps.

Extremely Thirsty Guy (ETG)

This type of guy will ask for a girl's number, or possibly on a date within the first couple messages. He tells the girl how beautiful she is, and the compliments never stop coming.

> **ETG:** *Wow you're gorgeous*
>
> **Girl:** *Oh thank you*
>
> **ETG:** *No problem. I'd love to take you to dinner sometime. Would you let me do that?*
>
> **Girl:** *Maybe, what were you thinking?*
>
> **ETG:** *Anywhere you want beautiful*
>
> **Girl:** **no response**

The girl usually stops responding after the first few messages because she gets a little creeped out with how thirsty one guy can be. For the most part, this guy doesn't do very well on Tinder, unless he meets an Extremely Thirsty Girl, who is a rare species in the Tinder world.

Extremely Witty Opener Guy (EWOG)

This guy has some really good openers that many would find hilarious. His messages are usually funny too, and he can carry a conversation fairly well. The problem is only certain types of girls appreciate these messages. Some girls find them to be too much, especially in the beginning, or they may not get the humor.

EWOG: I don't know who you are. I don't know what you want. If it's a hook up you're after, I can tell you I don't have that. But what I do have are a particular set of skills, skills that make me a delight for girls like you. If you hate my icebreaker, that will be the end of it. I will not look for you, I will not pursue you. But if you like my icebreaker, I may buy you coffee in the future :)

Girl: lmao okay Liam Neison

EWOG: your dog looks pretty cute. What's his name?

Sometimes these messages work out, sometimes they don't. For the girls they do work on, usually things are successful. EWOG does okay on Tinder.

Douchebag Guy (DBG)

This guy may do well at first, but at the first sign of rejection he starts making fun of the girl on her looks, personality, etc.

DBG: damn you're hot

Girl: oh why thank you :)

DBG: what's your sign?

Girl: I'm a taurus, wbu?

DBG: ohh a taurus, I heard taurus' are wild in the bedroom. Have you heard of "pegging"?

Girl: ummm yeah no thanks

DBG: I shouldn't even be talking to you, I'm way out of your league

While DBG does have some success, the first sign of rejection turns him into a craftsman tool, which then of course makes the girl uncomfortable, and ultimately ends the interaction. DBG needs to let some things roll off his back, possibly take a breather, and come back in a few days to try again. DBG is too emotional and has low self-esteem.

While there are obviously more types of "Tinder Guys," this does sum up a large majority of them. What all these guys have in common is they don't have much success on Tinder. The methods they use may work for a few girls, but not for the majority of girls whom they match with. Considering girls are into these guys enough to swipe right on their profile, the guys then just have to do enough to keep the attraction alive, and get said girl out onto a date. Unfortunately this does not happen for a majority of the girls they match with. Let's now go over a better persona to emulate, which I have named…

Fun Guy Who's a Challenge (FGWC)

FGWC: *Is that you in Paris in your second picture?*

Girl: *It is! I went last year with some friends*

FGWC: *Wow that's so exciting! What's your best memory from the trip?*

Girl: *I'd have to say visiting the Eiffel tower. You wouldn't believe how big it is.*

FGWC: Yeah I've never been to Paris before but always wanted to. You think I could go in your suitcase the next time you go there?

Girl: Lol, if you're okay being crammed next to a hair straightener and my underwear then sure

While this is just a brief example, FGWC is ultimately what we are going for in this book. I will go over much more detail as we progress, but FGWC has certain qualities that make him attractive to females on dating apps. He opens up with relevant a message, keeps the conversation exciting, but doesn't message the girl too much, thus making her wonder and think about him. This is so conversations don't get drawn out, and a high interest level from the female is maintained. She doesn't know exactly when he will message her, and he keeps her on the fence regarding his interest level. He's rather unpredictable and is a challenge when talking to girls on Tinder, while maintaining a fun, humorous persona. Before we go over this successful Tinder persona, we first need to go over why the previous types of guys, as well as a large majority of men on Tinder don't do as well as they could, and how to overcome these issues.

Why Many Guys Mess Up on Tinder

The reason a lot of guys mess up on Tinder is because they are one of the profiles I had previously mentioned, or a mix of them. Many guys send boring opener messages, which don't really do much to capture a girl's attention and make them want to start talking to them. They also send too many messages too often, pushing girls away as it makes them look needy and clingy. Then they may get mad or stop talking to girls at the first sign of rejection. FGWC changes all this. He sends girls an original opening message that isn't too over the top. He then keeps their interest via conversation, but doesn't message them constantly every day, making himself a challenge, thus making the girl miss him. He soon progresses to get their number or Snapchat ID, and sporadically messages them until eventually asking them on a date which they most likely agree to. Out of all the profiles, FGWC has the most success on Tinder because of the qualities he portrays. We'll be going over how to be a FGWC in the next chapter.

Part 4
Messaging Girls

Alright so you have matched with a girl and are ready to message her. I used to be a EWOG, and while some girls found me hilarious, others didn't respond. I think for some girls, it comes off as too over the top or they may not get the humor. You don't know what type of girl you are talking to before the opener, and like a comedian or band, you have to play to your audience. I would suggest waiting till you get a feel for the girl you are talking to, which would include analyzing the types of messages she sends you, before you start trying to joke with her.

There are two types of people that others are drawn to:

1. People who are like them.
2. People who they want to be.

This attraction is displayed in both relationships, as well as friendships. People like others who they have commonalities with. There is a married couple who I'm friends with on Facebook. They are constantly posting pictures and videos of themselves working out at the gym. They will take videos for each other, just to post on Facebook. While I find it rather annoying to constantly see videos of these two bozos working out in my time line, it reminds me of why they like each other and probably started dating in the first place; they have a shared interest. They both are obviously rather obsessed with exercise, and that may have helped draw them to each other. Whoever said opposites attract lived on a deserted island; commonalities attract. I mean imagine a republican and democrat dating each other, or an atheist and devout Christian? Do you think these relationships would work? While they can occasionally, studies have shown relationships with such opposing viewpoints usually don't last long.

I'm sure you've heard your grandma tell you to "just be yourself" when it comes to girls. While there is some truth to this, as you have to end up being yourself sooner or later, you can be a bit of a chameleon in the beginning. What I mean is go with the flow in the beginning, even if the girl brings something up that may not be your favorite. So let's say you matched with a girl who likes country music, but you're not a big fan. If she ever asks you if you like country music, say yes. Say you listen to it every now and then. You don't have to go out and buy a lifted truck and a Remington rifle, but you don't have to be a completely opposed to it either. Just kind of go with it in the beginning. This allows for commonality.

The First Message

If the girl matches with you, she obviously likes you somewhat, and wants to talk to you. Remember, girls have a TON of guys to choose between, and they are rather selective with their matches. Unless you're on Bumble, most girls don't message first; it's just the way society has been formed. For this reason, you will most likely be sending the first message.

With the first message, I would suggest using either their bio or pictures to start the conversation. It is something they can easily relate to, and is likely to get a response. Let me give you an example.

Let's say you match with a girl and in one her pictures she is hiking in Yellowstone Park. You could say:

Hiking is so relaxing! When did you visit Yellowstone?

Let's say she has a picture of herself snowboarding. You could say:

Snowboarding is so much fun! When was the first time you went?

Let's say she puts she loves tacos and sushi in your bio. You could ask:

What's your favorite place to get tacos?

To some this may seem elementary, but there's no reason to get too complicated when you don't have to. You can keep the first message simple. You're getting a feel for the girl. If there's not much to go on in the bio and pictures, I have a huge list of example openers you can use in Appendix A at the back of this book.

Something you do not want to do in the first message is put in a disqualifier. This would be something which alienates the girl, and makes her feel like she doesn't share commonalities with you. Let's back to the taco example. In the example before, I asked her what her favorite taco place is. I am waiting for her to give me an answer. I don't want to state alienating opinions before she even starts talking to me. Let me give you an example of a bad opener where you've noticed she eats tacos in one of her photos:

I'd have to say taco bell is the best taco place. I really hate Chipotle though. What's your favorite?

There are two problems with this opener. The first is she may hate taco bell, thus throwing things off kilter. While it's not terrible you love it, it doesn't help anything. But the second part is worse were you say you "hate Chipotle." Chipotle may very well be this girl's favorite restaurant. She could go to

Chipotle multiple times a week to get her fix. Chipotle could have given her a $100,000 scholarship to go to college. By stating you hate Chipotle, or country music, or the president in your messages or your bio, you are automatically alienating girls who could have been great matches. You don't want to do this. So let her talk first before you state your opinion. And even if you do hate Chipotle, you don't have to agree with her and say "Oh I love Chipotle too!" You don't have to say anything. You could just acknowledge her opinion and then continue the conversation.

Another bad opener is an assuming question. This can quickly paint you in a bad light, making you have to climb uphill to regain any chance you have left with this girl. Let's say in one of her pictures she is at the library. You feel she looks smart, and is probably a good student. Here's an assuming question:

Wow it looks like you're studying hard. I bet you're a nerd aren't you?

Making an assumption is never a good idea, especially when you are first getting to know someone. And while this is just one example, it could be anything. I bet you like trap music, I bet you're a gym junkie, I bet you etc. Assuming questions can get you into a hole, so it's best not to start any conversations with assuming questions.

After you have opened, you want to start conversing with her. The whole point of Tinder is to eventually get this girl on a date, and then possibly start dating her and/or playing horizontal poker. You cannot rush things though, as many girls are turned off by the "thirst" factor, which was touched on in Part 3 with the ETG profile. ETG's do not do well on Tinder, or with girls in general. For this reason I suggest taking things slow. Now there will be instances where the girl on the other end is constantly messaging you, possibly asking you to hang out, etc. Even in this scenario though, slower is better. Woman love a man who is a challenge. They long for a little bit of a chase and like guys whom they can't figure out. As in, guys who they think are "on the fence" about them.

If you've read my book *The Art of The Text* (**linkpony.com/text**), you're well aware of what I'm talking about here. So let's start with timing. You want to message girls back in the same amount of time or longer than they take to message you. Let's say you're talking to Sarah and she takes 3 hours to reply to your message on Tinder. You should wait 3 hours or longer to reply to her. If this girl doesn't think enough of you to respond right away, you have to do the same. Always use the amount of time she took to respond as a gauge of when to reply. Think about it like this; let's say she is taking 3 hours to reply to your messages and you are replying back the second you receive them. It looks rather "thirsty" from the girl's end of things, and this is a turn-off in female land. That's why taking your time to reply is important.

From Tinder, you are ultimately trying to get either her phone number or Snapchat ID. Tinder is not the place to ask this girl on a date. I repeat, Tinder *is not* the place to ask this girl on a date. Your best chance of getting a date with a girl from Tinder is after you two have built rapport together, she has gotten to know you a little, and she feels comfortable with you. You two have shared conversation, inside jokes, etc. This is when she will want to go out with you, and likely agree to a date. I have something to show you which I call "The Tinder Staircase."

The Tinder Staircase

Tinder

Snapchat and/or Phone

Go on a Date

Go on More Dates

Horizontal Poker

As you can see, there are levels you must reach before you get to the next step. If you try skipping a step in this staircase, you're chances of success will be greatly reduced.

While there is no set number, I would suggest sending a minimum of 7 messages (14 including her's) before asking for her phone number or Snapchat ID. And these are good messages, not "hey." Messages where you ask her opinion on things. Messages where you talk about her photos. Messages where you get to know her. Seven "hey's" does not count. Also, you should allow a minimum of one week from your first Tinder message before asking for her Snapchat or number. Again, this all goes back to not appearing too interested too soon. If you're using the advice I have laid out, it should take you at least a week to send seven messages. With that said, a good idea too is to put time in-between your messages. As in have a conversation with her one day, stop messaging her, and then wait 2 or 3 or 4 days before you send her another message.

Besides the openers, I can't give you specific messages to reply to this girl with. You're going to have to voyage on your own here, as every conversation is going to be different. I can however give you some tips on sending messages. Humor is always a good idea, and girls like guys who can make them laugh. So in your messages tease her, joke with her, and have fun. Another way to extend the conversation is through hooks. This is using the responses she gives you to keep the conversation alive. Let me give you an example:

Girl: I have two animals, a dog and a cat.

Guy: I love animals. What's your dog's name?

Girl: Simba

Guy: Ohh did you take that from Lion King?

Girl: Yes actually. I really liked that movie

Guy: I haven't watched that move in years. What's the last movie you watched?

In the example above I have underlined all the

hooks. Hooks are just phrases she puts in her messages which you can expand upon, and ask her questions about. This keeps the conversation alive, allowing you to talk with her more and keep building rapport. Using hooks, you can keep a conversation going for quite some time. Speaking of conversations though, you don't want to be talking to this girl all day. Even if she is sending you messages back right away, and providing excellent responses, you still want her to miss you. For this reason, after sending some messages back and forth, stop talking to her. Sometimes I say "gtg", other times I just reply to her question days later. This is part of being a challenge. You don't want to be too available for this girl.

Something else to remember is most people like talking about themselves, which includes things they are good at, their field of study, their job, and accomplishments they've made in their life. Most people, including girls, think the world revolves around themselves. There's been studies which found pleasurable chemicals are released in the brain when people talk about themselves; it makes them feel good. Knowing this, you should try to keep the conversation focused around the girl and get her to open up about herself. Don't talk about yourself too often unless specifically asked by her, but even then, try and get the conversation back to being focused around her. Again, things that someone would be proud of are great conversation topics such as their accomplishments, recent trips, their job, etc.

Dale Carnegie has said in his book *How to Win Friends and Influence People*, "A person's name is to that person, the sweetest, most important sound in any language." People like hearing their own name. Knowing this, you should bring up the girl you're talking to name in conversation every now and again. This will help to make her feel more attracted to you.

So while giving you some tips on items to talk about, I also want to go over items you should NOT partake in or talk about, at least not in the very beginning of messaging her. These would include:

- *Anything sexual, such as asking her favorite position, bra size, etc.*
- *Asking if she wants you to send her a d*** pic (I still don't get why some guys do this).*
- *Anything about politics or religion.*
- *Messaging her too frequently without sufficient responses or time in-between.*
- *Adding her on Facebook, Instagram, or any other social media platform the second you match with her.*

Most girls do not like talking about anything sexual until they've at least gotten to know a guy a little bit. Asking sexual questions too soon can be a big turn off for girls. And then I'm sure you've heard this before, but politics and religion are taboo too, at least until you've gotten to know her a little better. If you two have differing opinions things can get heated and diminish your chances of going out with her again.

I've mentioned it frequently throughout this book and will most likely mention it again; challenge. I want you to remember that word, because that is what will make you successful with women on Tinder and beyond. Messaging her too frequently and adding her on social media too quickly is the opposite of challenge. Stick to the timing principle I had mentioned before, and sometimes stop messaging her for a few days before continuing the conversation. Also, there is no reason to add her on any social media platform until at least the second date.

After conversing with girls on Tinder, I used to go for the number, however I've come to like asking for their Snapchat more now. The reason being is because many girls love attention, and thus post stories of themselves dancing in their car, watching TV, or whatever else their daily life involves. As I said before, most people think the earth revolves around them. This is excellent material to use for more conversations with said girl. Considering you still don't know her that well, when you only have her number, you are grasping for straws with what to text her. If you have her Snapchat however, and see she is at a Post Malone concert on her Snapchat story, you can start asking her questions such as what her favorite Post Malone song is, how close to the stage she was, how the concert was, etc. It allows for much more conversation material.

If the girl you're talking to has a Snapchat will depend on her age. Almost all of Generation Z and millennial girls will have Snapchats, however if you are talking to women older than this, the percentage may differ. In this case you just have to go for the phone number, and make use with it.

To ask for the Snapchat ID (or phone number), just be direct; you don't need a cheesy line. Here is an example after sending at least seven messages (and at least one week has gone by) with a girl you're talking to on Tinder:

> **Girl:** *Yes you're right, the Van Allen radiation belt would have prevented any astronauts from going to the moon. You're too funny!*
>
> **Guy:** *I told you so! You have a Snapchat?*
>
> **Girl:** *Yea, it's beckysue81.*
>
> **Guy:** *Cool, I'll message you on there later.*

Here's an example with a phone number:

> **Girl:** *12 inches?*
>
> **Guy:** *Yup!*
>
> **Girl:** *Wow, I had no idea turtles could grow to that size.*
>
> **Guy:** *The animal world is a crazy place. Hey I'm about to go eat dinner, but think I could get your*

number before I do?
Girl: *525-889-1132*
Guy: *Thanks, ttyl*

I like to ask for the number or Snapchat ID towards the end of a conversation. I feel it makes things less awkward, as you can get it from the girl and not feel obligated to continue messaging on Tinder. This is why I put in an "out" as I did in the example above, where I say "I'm about to go eat dinner." This way the girl isn't expecting another message back after she gives me her number or Snap ID.

After ending the conversation, I suggest waiting until at least the next day to message her via Snapchat or text message. This keeps her on her toes, as opposed to immediately messaging her on Snapchat the moment she sends you her Snap ID. This makes you more of a challenge, a needed component of a male who is successful with women.

Are these lines simple? Yes, they are. But do they work? Yes, they do. As long as you have built rapport, and you can tell this girl is into on Tinder, then just directly asking for her number or Snapchat ID is fine, and a fancy line isn't needed. Here's the thing, if you talk to a girl on Tinder for a while, and for some reason she isn't into you, no fancy line is going to get her number. You could come up with an extremely humorous line that will make her laugh, but if she doesn't like you, she's not going to give you her number. That's why it's a good idea to wait until you feel she shows signs of interest before asking for her number or Snap ID. What are signs of interest?

- *Any type of emoji in her messages.*
- *Messages which are of equal length to yours.*
- *She is asking you questions.*
- *She initiates a conversation.*
- *She responds quickly to your messages.*

If on the other hand she is showing you signs of disinterest, you definitely do not want to ask for her number, and maybe can ask for her Snapchat. What are signs of disinterest?

- *Sending one word answers.*
- *Taking days to responds*
- *Completely ignoring your messages.*
- *No emoticons.*
- *Not asking any questions.*

If a girl is displaying signs of disinterest, it doesn't mean you're out for the count. I've had girls who showed all these signs, but I was able to get their Snapchat ID and eventually onto a date. Some girls take a little more warming up to than others, some girls are nervous, some girls are busy, etc. You don't know exactly what they are thinking. For this reason, if you really like a girl and she is showing signs of disinterest, it's best to go only for the Snapchat, not the number. I would compare Snapchat to Facebook, in terms of how accepting girls are to friending guys. Girls are much more willing to give out their Snapchat ID versus their phone number, as the number more of a personal effect. For this reason, even if a girl has a low interest level in you, she may be willing to give you her Snapchat, and time may help you win her over.

Once you get her Snapchat ID and add her, immediately change the settings to keep messages for 24 hours. As you already know, if you don't change the settings Snapchat immediately deletes your conversation as soon as you send it or read it. I can't tell you how many times I went about my day and completely forgot what I sent a girl, to which I got a reply message to hours later. Having the Snaps saved for 24 hours saves you from the awkward "what did I ask you again" message.

Part 5
Getting a Date

You have matched with a girl on Tinder, sent some messages, got her Snapchat, and have been conversing with her for a little while. You feel rapport has been built, she is into you, and you're ready to ask her on a date. Wonderful!

When asking a girl on a date, you want to pick a day that is at least 2+ days out (e.g. It's Monday. Ask for a date on Wednesday or beyond). This is so you don't seem too eager, going back to the challenge aspect. When you ask her for a date, you want to have a time and location picked in advance. You are not asking her "what do you want to do?" Girls like it when guys take the lead and have plans made. A great first date is either coffee or ice cream. This date is cheap and allows for easy conversation. What I've found with Tinder is unfortunately some girls do not look like their profile pictures or have the personality you thought they did. They may have gained a ton of weight, are annoying, contracted malaria, etc. For this reason, it's possible you might not like this girl, and you might realize that soon after you meet her. Coffee or ice cream will cost you $5 and an hour of your time, and you can then delete her profile and carry on with your life. If you set up a limo driven steak dinner for the first date and Shrek shows up at the restaurant, you will be out a lot of money on a girl you have no intention of continuing to talk to.

On the other hand, if you do like this girl and the date is going well, you can always extend it and go somewhere after the coffee. This would include a restaurant, park, arcade, etc. This is why a cheap first date is your best option. Let's go over an example of a text to send for the first date. This message will be sent via Snapchat or text message, not on Tinder. You should be past Tinder by the first date message.

Guy: Hey Sarah. You free Thursday night? We should get coffee together.

Girl: Yeah, I can do Thursday. Where did you want to go?

Guy: Giovanni's café on Riverdale. Text me your address, I'll pick you up at 7pm on Thursday.

Girl: 182 Easy St, Hightown, PA

Guy: Cool, see ya Thursday!

This example is a best case scenario. Obviously as we know with women, things don't always go perfectly. A good idea is to pick her up for this first date. This is because it leads to a better chance of getting a first kiss at the end of the night. Some girls, especially ones you don't know that well, may not be comfortable with you picking them up for the first date. So if they ask you to meet them there instead, just agree as this is fine.

If the girl says she is busy but gives you an alternate day to meet, this is a good sign. She most likely is busy that day, as she is offering to meet you another time. Find a day that works for both of you and go on the date then.

With Friends

What if she offers for you to go out with her and her friends? Turn it down! This is one of the most awkward evenings you will ever experience and will not help build attraction between you and your date. If you have ever accepted this in the past, you know what I'm talking about here. Let's say you hypothetically did accept this date though. You would end up meeting her and her 2 or 3 or 4 friends by yourself. You would stand there awkwardly as they gossiped about items you know nothing about. You're in essence the 3rd or 4th or 5th wheel in this scenario. Then at the end of the night you might get a hug from this girl, and your evening will end. It's never a good idea, especially for the first date, to go out with her friends. So if she offers this, turn it down and reschedule to go out with her alone, on a day you're both free.

The only exception to this would be a double date. As in if she is going out with one of her single girl friends, and you and one of your single guy friends meet them somewhere. This scenario is much better, as you have someone you know there (your guy friend), and you both can split up at the end of the night for personal one-on-one time.

During the Date and After

I don't go into much detail on what to do during the date or after, as this book is focused on matching and communicating with girls on dating apps. In my new book *How to Attract Women* (linkpony.com/women) I do go over this, what to do if she says maybe or no to a date, as well as much more in regards to attracting females and the female psyche. The link above will bring you to that book. I highly recommend you check it out!

Conclusion

Our book has come to an end. With the knowledge provided, you now have the tools to attract and go out with good looking, high quality women you meet on Tinder, Bumble, or any other dating app or website. Remember the Tinder staircase and the information I have laid out for you. Use this book as a reference, and come back to it when you need help talking to girls. Using this book, *The Art of the Text*, *How to Attract Women*, my free special report *Subconscious Attraction*, and the free advice on my website <u>GetMoreDates.com</u>, your dating life will improve exponentially.

For extra help, I also have a "VIP Coaching" section on my website where I offer more tailored advice to help you personally attract women. Good luck in you pursuit of women! I wish you the best.

Appendix A, which contains 80 example opener messages, can be found on page 63.

How to Attract Women

The Last of the Dating Books You'll Ever Need to Get the Girls You've Always Wanted

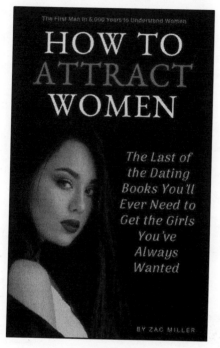

Link to Amazon Page:
linkpony.com/women

Girls have been a mystery for thousands of years however one man has finally figured them out. In *How to Attract Women*, author Zac Miller goes over the entire process of attracting women. Appearance, conversation topics, psychological techniques, body language, and much more… it's all included in this book! **You can** be with the girl of your dreams! Find out how now in *How to Attract Women*.

The Art of The Text
The Ultimate Guide on Texting Girls

Shortened Link to Amazon Page
linkpony.com/text

Do you struggle with texting girls? All this can be solved with *The Art of the Text*. Zac Miller takes your hand and shows you exactly what to text girls to have them begging to be with you. All the secrets are spilled in this tell all guide. Learn how to text girls now!

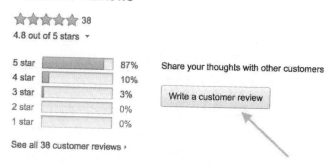

If you are enjoying this book, could you please leave a review on Amazon? It would be greatly appreciated and allow me to come out with more informative books in the future. A shortened link to the review page is below:

Linkpony.com/match

Appendix A: Conversation Openers

- Where are you from?
- What do you do for a living?
- Do you have any pets?
- Are you a vegetarian?
- What did you do last weekend? Anything fun?
- What's your sign? Do you believe in star signs?
- Do you know what Chinese zodiac you are?
- What's your family like?
- What's your favorite cocktail? Do you have a signature drink?
- What's your normal weekend like?
- Are you a competitive person?
- Are you a morning person or a night owl?
- Do you like scary movies?
- What do you like to do in your downtime?
- Would you consider yourself a sarcastic person?
- Do you like tattoos?
- What's something you could talk about for hours?
- What's a typical day in your life like?
- If you could live anywhere, where would it be?
- If you could be a character in any movie, who would you be?

- What actor/actress would play you in the movie of your life?

- What's one thing I should know about you that's not on your profile?

- How did you pick your Snapchat name?

- What's your middle name?

- What's one saying you try to live by?

- Do you have any tattoos? If you got one what would you get?

- Are you close to your family?

- If you could choose a superpower what would it be?

- What's the nerdiest thing you're willing to admit?

- What are you most likely to stay up all night talking about?

- I love hearing other people's stories. Do you have a good one to tell?

- What's your idea of the perfect day?

- When you were a kid, what did you want to be when you grew up?

- Are you an adventurous person?

- What's your favorite restaurant?

- Would you describe yourself as a romantic person?

- Yes or no: Do you like to dance?

- Yes or no: Do you believe in love at first sight?

- Yes or no: Are you romantic?
- Do you have any nicknames?
- Where did you grow up?
- Are you an outgoing person or are you on the shy side?
- What's one thing you'd bring with you to a deserted tropical island?
- What's the fondest memory you have?
- What's your favorite place in the whole world?
- Tell me one random fact about yourself.
- If you had one wish from a genie, what would you wish for?
- See any good movies lately?
- Read any good books lately?
- I'm a big exerciser. Do you like working out?
- I'm into the outdoors. Do you like hiking?
- Where's the last place you visited?
- Do you like to travel?
- Do you have any plans for a vacation this year?
- What kind of music do you usually listen do?
- What's the last concert you went to?
- I love music. What the first song or album you ever got?
- What game on your phone do you play the most?
- What shows do you binge watch?

- What's your favorite way to relax?
- What's your favorite sports team?
- I'm a big sports fan. Do you like watching games?
- Are you a gardener? I love working outside.
- I'm a big foodie. What's your favorite restaurant in the area?
- I love the outdoors. Are you a camper?
- I love a good road trip. What was the last one you went on?
- What type of stuff do you like to do on the weekend?
- What kinds of things do you like to do for fun?
- What do you like to do when you go out?
- What type of stuff do you do in your spare time?
- What's your favorite book?
- What's one city you want to travel to?
- What's your favorite band?
- What's your favorite movie?
- What's one great book you've recently read?
- Do you like working out?
- What's your favorite TV show?
- Do you have any hobbies you're passionate about?
- Are you an outdoorsy person?
- Do you play any sports?

Made in the USA
Coppell, TX
23 August 2021